# Four Pals in a Parade

(An Adventure with Friends who are Different)

# By Angel Tucker, C.H.B.C

Illustrated by Steve Pileggi

# Four Pals in a Parade

By Angel Tucker, C.H.B.C

Illustrated by Steve Pileggi

## MASCOT® BOOKS

www.mascotbooks.com

For more information, please contact:
Mascot Books
560 Herndon Parkway
Herndon, VA 20170
info@mascotbooks.com

Library of Congress Control Number: 2015912782

CPSIA Code: PRLS1015A
ISBN-13: 9781631773631

Printed in the United States

# ACKNOWLEDGMENTS
## For "Four Pals™" Series 2

First, I'd like to thank God, who is the creator of ALL things – including our personalities! I'm so thankful we are all different! Just think how crazy the world would be if we were all the same!

Next, I'd like to thank my husband, Dennis, for being so supportive of the development of these books and encouraging me when I thought they would never get finished! Also, to my five children, who have kept me from ever having a dull moment! I love and appreciate each of these little personalities!

A huge thank you to Steve Pileggi, illustrator of this series, for his creativity and ability to make the stories come alive! Much was asked of him, and he came through with flying colors! He is truly amazing!

Thanks to Mascot Books for your assistance in developing Series 2 of the *Four Pals*. The results are nothing short of spectacular and I am happy to have you as part of our success.

Last, but certainly not least, words cannot begin to express my thanks to the Personality Insights team. Dr. Robert A. Rohm was a tremendous help in getting the first series of the *Four Pals* to print and is someone I consider a mentor and a friend. Pedro Gonzalez was instrumental in making sure our graphics were beautiful and was always willing to assist when asked. I enjoy working with Personality Insights on a regular basis to spread the word about the benefits of understanding personality types!

Angel Tucker
C.H.B.C.
National Speaker/Trainer
Best-Selling Author
Award Winning Author
Winner of "50 Great Writers You Should be Reading"

Learn more about Angel and the Four Pals, as well as her other books at:
personalityprofiles.org or fourpalsfanclub.com

# Welcome to the
# "Four Pals"™
## Series!

These books were created for three reasons:

1. To show children that God is the creator of everything – even our personalities!

2. To teach children all about the different personality types!

3. To let children know that it's okay to feel unique and special as well as be different from their friends!

Here is a further description of each of the personality types. This should assist you in giving your children a better idea of how God made each of us different. The important fact to remember is that all children have a unique blend of ALL FOUR of these personality styles. No one will fit neatly into one style. All children will possess some of all of these traits and will exhibit each of the four different types of behavior at different times. Usually, however, one style will emerge as the most predominant trait and this will be the trait the child will demonstrate most often. It will also be the trait that he or she will be most comfortable using on a daily basis. We often say, "That is the way they are wired!"

# David

DAVID is our wonderful "D" type personality! The letter "D" represents the word "**Dominant**." "D" type personalities love to be in charge and have things done their way. "D"s think fast and move fast! Their communication style is bottom line. Their attitude is lead, follow, or get out of my way! You never have to wonder what a "D" is thinking - they will just tell you! "D" children are usually the ones leading all the group activities and telling all the other kids what they will be doing. God bless the **Outgoing/Task-Oriented "D"** type personality!

# Iris

**IRIS** is our wonderful "**I**" type personality! The letter "**I**" represents the word "**Inspiring.**" "**I**" type personalities love to have fun! They are very optimistic and outgoing! They tend to be forgetful at times because they are usually in a hurry to do things! They also move fast! Their communication style is exciting and enthusiastic. They don't do well with lots of details and information and may have difficulty accomplishing tasks because they lose their focus. They love being around other people, thrive on attention and love to entertain others! God bless the **Outgoing/People-Oriented** "**I**" type personality!

# Summer

**SUMMER** is our wonderful "**S**" type personality! The letter "**S**" represents the word "**Supportive.**" "**S**" type personalities are very compliant and pleasant. They do not like conflict. They like peace and harmony. They sometimes have trouble making decisions because they tend to make up their minds slowly. Their communication style is "easy-going." In other words, they tend to adapt easily to whatever is going on around them in their environment. They love people and relationships! "**S**"s love being around other people and helping everyone they meet. They are sensitive and sometimes get their feelings hurt easily. They like to feel appreciated and secure. God bless the **Reserved/People-Oriented** "**S**" type personality!

# Charlie

**CHARLIE** is our wonderful "*C*" type personality! The letter "*C*" represents the word "**Cautious.**" "*C*" type personalities enjoy having a routine and schedule. They are usually very good students and like things that challenge their mind. Their communication style is A to Z, which means that, details and planning are very important to a "*C*." That is why they ask so many questions. The "*C*" type personality prefers to do things that have been planned out especially if it involves a large group of people. They are very comfortable being alone and working independently. They appreciate quality more than quantity. God bless the **Reserved/Task-Oriented** "*C*" type personality!

The "**Four Pals**" series is designed to have 1 book in each series that highlights each of the four different personality styles. To find other "**Four Pals**" books, visit: www.FourPalsFanClub.com or www.personalityprofiles.org

David, Iris, Summer, and Charlie were all in their class at Tuckerville Elementary School. It was just about time to leave for the day when the teacher, Mrs. Solomon, made an announcement. "Attention class," she began. "I have some exciting news." The students listened closely as the teacher explained. "Next Saturday is the birthday of our town. Tuckerville was established on that date in 1969. To celebrate, our town will have a parade. Our class was chosen to decorate and ride on the school float!"

Each of the four friends felt differently about this announcement. David hoped he could be in charge of the project and tell everyone else what to do. Iris was excited about riding on a colorful float and hoped there would be candy to throw. Summer felt so special that her class was chosen to participate in the parade, but she also felt a little sorry for the other classes. Charlie was glad the teacher gave them plenty of notice so he would have time to research how to make a float.

"Can I be in charge?" asked David.

"Will there be candy to throw?" questioned Iris.

"What are the exact measurements of the float?" inquired Charlie.

"David, you can help me guide the students. Iris, there will be candy and yes, you can throw it. Charlie, I will get that information to you by tomorrow. I know how much you like to plan so I am counting on you to put all our ideas into a final sketch."

"Mrs. Solomon," Summer said softly. "I am happy to help in any way that you need me. It is wonderful that our class was chosen and I want to make sure everyone has a good time creating the float." Mrs. Solomon was glad that Summer was willing to help, wherever she was needed. Summer was always such a good helper. "Tomorrow we will discuss everyone's ideas for the float, so think about what you would like to do," said their teacher.

Iris knew she didn't need to think about it. She wanted lots of flowers and stars, and a colored banner that read, "Happy Birthday, Tuckerville!"

10

David knew what he wanted, too. He wanted the float to be the
biggest one in the parade!

Summer didn't care what was on the float as long as she was able to spend time with her classmates. She loved spending time with people, especially her friends. She couldn't wait to see what they could accomplish when they worked together as a team.

Charlie knew exactly what he needed to do...research! He was going to head straight for the library after school.

The next day, each of the students shared their ideas and Charlie took detailed notes. Mrs. Solomon also gave him the measurements of the float just as she promised. Charlie only had three days to study all of the ideas from the class and prepare the sketch. After that, it would be time to decorate the float so it would be ready for the parade next Saturday. He was happy that he would have the entire weekend to work on it. Plus, they were out of school Monday for a teacher planning day. Charlie would have three whole days to draw the sketch just right. He liked things to be correct.

It was finally Tuesday and Charlie had created the most awesome sketch ever. The other kids were amazed that he did such a good job. Summer was so grateful that he spent three entire days working on the sketch to help the class. Summer loved teamwork. Now they would be able to create a beautiful float for the parade!

Summer brought cookies and juice boxes for everyone to share. She thought her friends would enjoy a nice snack. Summer was always thinking of others and enjoyed doing nice things. She decided not to tell the others about the surprise until Mrs. Solomon said it was time for a break. She didn't want to upset the teacher with everyone eating when they should be working on the float.

After they worked on the float for about an hour, Mrs. Solomon suggested they take a break. Summer pulled the cookies and juice boxes from her backpack and let everyone know she had brought a snack for all of them. David was the first one to get a cookie and looked for the one with the most chocolate chips.

Iris was especially excited to see the snack. "Oh, cookies!" she squealed with delight. "And, they're my favorite kind." Charlie made sure he used anti-bacterial soap on his hands before he carefully chose a cookie. He wouldn't want to eat germs! Charlie did not like germs.

Summer made sure everyone chose a cookie and then she offered one to her teacher before she ate one. Her teacher gladly took a cookie and thanked Summer for being so thoughtful. This made Summer very happy.

Before they knew it, the float was complete. Summer thought it looked beautiful! The class had decided to decorate the float in red, white, and blue. There were gold stars and white flowers. There was a big banner that read, "Happy Birthday Tuckerville" in blue letters. Summer made sure there were enough seats on the float for all of them. As Charlie pointed out during their design plan, it would be safer for them to sit instead of stand.

Finally, it was Saturday! All of the friends took their places on the float. David took the seat at the front of the float and Iris jumped for the seat closest to the candy. Summer decided that she would ride on the float until the parade began, then she would walk beside the float. That way kids would not get too close and get hurt.

Once they were all in place, the driver started towards their place in line with the other floats. The entire parade route was decorated for the celebration and all the floats looked so festive! The streets were lined with thousands of people who lived in Tuckerville.

David checked out the other floats to see if his school's was the biggest. So far, he didn't see any that were bigger. Iris looked through the candy. She was excited that they had lots of different kinds to throw. Summer waited for the float to come to a stop and asked the driver if it was safe for her to walk beside the float now. Charlie regularly reminded Iris to stay in her seat so she didn't fall off the float.

It was time for the parade to begin! Music from the middle school band in the front of the line started to play and the floats all rolled down Chase Street. David waved to everyone who watched the parade and was glad he was up front. Iris had a blast throwing the candy and enjoyed watching the kids try to catch it. Summer walked beside the float and was thankful that everyone was so happy. Charlie refilled the candy bucket for Iris whenever it was almost empty.

The parade was finally over. Summer was sad to see the day come to an end but was also thankful that they were able to participate in the parade. She loved creating memories with her friends. This was something she would remember for a long time.

Once they reached the school parking lot, it was time to remove all of the decorations from the float. David hoped it didn't take very long. He thought "un-decorating" sounded kind of boring. Iris wasn't crazy about the idea either. She liked doing things that were fun and that didn't sound fun to her at all. Summer assured Iris that she would help and they would be done in no time!

Charlie announced that he already knew they would have to take all the decorations off the float and he had designed a plan that would accomplish this in the most efficient manner. Everyone looked over his plans and they all got to work.

27

In what seemed like no time at all, they were finished. Iris was so happy that it didn't take very long. David announced that he was headed to the park if anyone wanted to join him. He kept a close eye on everyone to make sure no one started running towards the park before him. David liked to be first at everything!

Summer thanked David for the invitation, but she had already promised her mother she would help around the house after the parade. Summer always kept her promises. Charlie reminded David that Saturday was the day he cleaned his room and he had already re-arranged his schedule for the parade so he needed to go home as well.

Suddenly, everyone heard the teacher say, "Before anyone leaves, I have some exciting news." They all listened as she explained. "In a few weeks, we will go on a field trip. We are all going to visit the aquarium!"

All of the friends were excited to hear this news! The aquarium was new and none of them had a chance to go yet. David exclaimed, "Woo hoo! I get to skip school AND go to the aquarium. Awesome!" Iris said, "I am bringing my new camera and I hope they have sea cucumbers. I have always wanted to touch one."

Charlie had no intention of touching a slimy sea cucumber, but he couldn't wait to learn more about the various animals at the aquarium. He decided he would look at the aquarium's website to see what they had so he could read about them before they went. Summer couldn't wait to see how they fed the animals.

"I'm so glad God made us all friends even though we all like different things," Summer said with a huge smile on her face. Her friends agreed and they all looked forward to their next adventure together.

# Reader's Guide

This is Book 3 in this series. The focus in this book is on Summer – the Supportive "S" type personality! To find more Four Pals books, go to www.FourPalsFanClub.com or www.personalityprofiles.org.

## David

Did you see how David wanted to be first at everything? This is because he tends to be competitive and wants to be in front of everyone else. His style is also task-oriented rather than people-oriented. Sometimes his desire to be faster than others and get his way can hurt peoples' feelings or make others not like him. He needs to remember to consider the feelings of others. David is a great friend to have, especially when it comes to striving to be the best!

## Iris

Did you notice how Iris loved to interact with people? She is energized by others! Iris loves to be involved in everything that is going on around her! She isn't very interested in doing things she considers boring though. Sometimes she can be forgetful in nature, especially when she is having a good time! Iris is a great friend to have, especially when it comes to making sure everyone has lots of fun!

## Charlie

Did you notice how Charlie loved to plan? He enjoys learning and planning to make sure that everything is efficient and works well! He isn't fond of "going with the flow" or doing things without thinking them through first. Sometimes his need to have a plan and schedule can prevent him from having fun. Charlie is a great friend, especially when you need someone you can count on!

## Summer

Did you notice how Summer enjoyed making others happy? She loves spending time with friends and creating special memories. She also likes to make others feel special too! She also makes sure she does what she says she will do so others can count on her! Sometimes her trusting style can allow people to take advantage of her. Summer is a great friend especially when you need to share your thoughts and feelings with someone.

# About the Author

Angel Tucker is a Certified Human Behavior Consultant, International Speaker/Trainer, Best-Selling Author, Award-Winning Author, Expert Personality Profiler, Air Force Spouse, and mom! She has over 23 years of experience as a professional speaker. She feels blessed to be able to share her knowledge of personality types with others and has trained tens of thousands of people on the benefits of understanding our differences. Angel loves the Four Pals and views them as "real kids" in many ways! She enjoys writing about their adventures together as friends, even though they are all different.

In her spare time, Angel enjoys traveling, cross-stitching, listening to Christian music, and hanging out with her family. If you are interested in having Angel speak at your next engagement, please contact her using the following information:

Website: www.personalityprofiles.org

Email: personalitypro@msn.com

Twitter: @PersonalityDr

Facebook: Personality Profiles LLC

The "Four Pals" series is designed to have 1 book in each series that highlights one of the personality styles.
To find out more, go to:

www.personalityprofiles.org
or
www.fourpalsfanclub.com

## Look for our other "Four Pals" books:
*Four Pals at the Park*
*Four Pals at the Zoo*
*Four Pals at a Party*
*Four Pals in a Science Class*
*Four Pals at the Pool*
*Four Pals at the Circus*
*Four Pals on a Field Trip*

For an autographed copy, visit Angel Tucker at
www.personalityprofiles.org